G000117173

[

AMBUSH

Nigel Jenkins

To Juri, sound man
supreme, with warm thanks,

GOMER

First Impression—1998

ISBN 1 85902 568 4

© Nigel Jenkins

Nigel Jenkins has asserted his right under the Copyright,
Designs and Patents Act, 1988, to be identified as Author of this Work.

All rights reserved. No part of this book may be reproduced, stored in a
retrieval system, or transmitted in any form or by any means, electronic,
electrostatic, magnetic tape, mechanical, photocopying, recording or
otherwise without permission in writing from the publishers, Gomer
Press, Llandysul, Ceredigion.

This book is published with the support of the
Arts Council of Wales.

Printed in Wales at
Gomer Press, Llandysul, Ceredigion

To
Robin Campbell,
for the redirection 'outward home'.

ACKNOWLEDGEMENTS

Acknowledgements are due to the following in which some of these poems first appeared:

The New Welsh Review, Planet, The New Statesman (England), BBC Wales, Poetry Wales, Lyric (India), Swansea City Council, Scintilla, Red Poets Society, The Western Mail, Menna Elfyn's Eucalyptus (Gwasg Gomer, 1995), The Haiku Quarterly (England), Radical Wales, Border Country (ed. David Hart, 1991), SWAG, Intimate Portraits (Seren/Glynn Vivian Art Gallery, 1995), HTV's series A Word in Your Eye (January-February, 1997), Y Drych (USA), Trying the Line, A volume of tribute to Gillian Clarke (ed. Menna Elfyn, 1997), Say That Again (eds. Mairwen Jones and John Spink, Pont, 1997).

The author gratefully acknowledges the award of a bursary from the Arts Council of Wales which bought him time to work on these poems.

CONTENTS

I

(Please fill in name, weight and height)

I, ..., a tensioned heap
of water, calcium, organic compounds,
weighing .... stone
and standing, for now, ... feet tall

blink out from the boneroom
at what little of the all,
and seem, as I stare,
less than a
less than a photon of starshine.

I, like you, am atom matter
born of stars dead, remassed and re-
shattered, through aeons flung
to lodge awhile in a sun's, the Sun's realm
as iron for blood, calcium for teeth,

every molecule of my DNA
as plenous with atoms as the galaxy with stars.

My boot, to be sure, is death to the worm,
I am fifty million million cells.
Yet, like an atom, I am all but void:
switch off my electricity
and—dis-charged the repulsions that bind me—
I crumble to a fine invisible dust.
Like an atom, like you, like a galaxy
I am almost wholly empty space,

vessel and witness of the vastitudes.

The Cosmic Gnomes

1.

Fossilized light; nothing disappears
Though all is rearranged.
Lost are they who are unamazed.

Tân mwyn-ddoe; ni diflanna dim
Er ailosodir oll.
Y sawl heb sêl, sydd ar goll.

2.

Blasted light; stardust are we, luxivores—
The cosmos conscious grown:
Primed for voyage outward home.

Tân ffrwyd-wyllt; lwch sêr, ym hil derwyn
Ymwybodol-cosmos-bryf,
Yn barod, allfyned, adref.

3.

Pulsing light; supernovae tune the Earth;
Atoms dance, atoms sing.
They kill, die who seek to cling.

Tân cur calon; supernovae'n tiwnio'r Tir;
Dawns atomau, cân atomau;
A laddo, ei grafanc, angau.

4.

Onward light; a quasar's gleam, aeons dead,
A face's in a glass:
We gaze always on the past.

Rhagddo dân; lleu cwasar, aeonau crin,
Wyneb yn y drych sy'n rhoi:
In drem fythol ar ein doe.

5.

Dizzying light; more suns than the billions
Whom we starve as we feast.
If all gave, all would receive.

Tân rhoi pendro; heuliau mwy na'r myrdd
A lwgwn wrth in wledda.
O roi dogn, pob un a rodia.

6.

Milk light; we slay the whale yet outsight crave,
Intelligence returned.
Mind's self-survival mind yearns.

Tân maeth-laeth; lladd morfil, encilio'r awch
Adennill ein deall:
Cof goroesi, cof y call.

7.

Measured light; atoms, star-built, grown to know
Space in us, we in space.
Cosmos observed, cosmos changed.

Mesuredig dân; atomau, ystum sêr, diwygio dysg
Gofod ynom, ninnau mewn gofod.
O nodi'r cosmos, newidia'r hanfod.

8.

Finalizing light; an eye to the stars,
A foot in primal slime.
We change * con\sider * or die.

Tân y terfyn; trem ar y sêr,
Troi ein traed mewn llaid.
Gwella * pwylla * neu marw sy raid.

[Welsh versions by Menna Elfyn]

14

ATOM I

! and all, for all a numberless age,
was heat's whole and lightless light

until, radiant, the oneness cooled
and night's inventors, the atoms, danced

dreaming stars and dreaming
the eyes to see them.

ATOM II

Indivisible?
Take an apple, take a knife,
slice the fruit in two,
halve and halve again
until, times ninety, you approach

the irreducible:

a little know-how, a
steady hand, and—Hiroshima!—
the at

        om
           's yours.

We'll dig iron on the asteroids, mine
awe in the electron.
We particle, we thing,
we jerk into name
the halves of nothing, makers still
of mere history;

unloved the wave, the flesh
unpleasured.

THE CREATION

When God clocked off from work one day,
    Having put the finishing touches to Wales,
The Archangel Gabriel begged the Creator
    To divest His opus of some of its veils.

'She's the finest,' said God, 'of all my creations,
    A land of quite extraordinary charms,
From her alpine peaks and salmon-packed streams
    To her golden coast with its prosperous farms.

'Her people I have blessed with laverbread and cockles
    Cwrw Felinfoel and great mineral wealth,
They'll be wizards of rugby, singers and bards,
    And they'll speak the language of heaven itself.'

'But haven't you, Boss,' the Archangel demurred,
    'Haven't you somewhat overpaid 'em?'
'Not,' replied God with a devilish smirk,
    'Not if you look at the neighbours I've made 'em.'

THE ELEVENTH COMMANDMENT

'And Moses,' said God, 'I almost forgot:
    For Wales, a land that's so devout,
I think we should add one more to the list:
    'Thou shalt not, ye sinners, be found out.'

OBSERVATORY

A cloudless night:
and we have come, the public,
to peer at the stars
from a dome in the cowfields.
Impatient kids orbit
the parental queue; they
manifest now and then
in a gloom of red light
that spills from within
across the sludgy turf.
Though we are less to a star
than half a twitch of a gnatlet's wing,
we wait what seems
a long cold hour
to slot briefly inside
with the 'scope and some words
of professional awe.
One of time's younger assassins,
chasing through the dark,
trips and takes a fall—
'Rhodri,' comes a voice,
'You are here, boy, to consider
the cosmos, not to go
flailing around in the mud.'

SUDDENLY

Grey mid March her bikeride home;
daily the heave against wind's denial,
the drowning daily of seabird and wave
by the drone relentless rush-time cars.

What then raised her eye
—zigzag skewed in the bundling grey—
was a fiery squiggle of sun-struck cloud.

And that cloud, she knew, that cloud that moment
could change, in ways, a person's life,
could change, once observed, the universe.

VENUS

Of like age and girth, of chiming
constitution, I, careless Earth, am
your tricksy sister, flattered indeed
—queen of the twilights—
to blaze for your fancy
beauty's banner, love's name.

Those, yes, the glory days
when you dreamed for me,
veiled beneath inviolate cloud,
triassic prairies, swamps
of steamy innocence . . .
Gwener, Ishtar, Tai-Pe . . .

Then, to my truth, your penetration:
the oven-blast breath of CO_2,
the skin that melts lead,
the tears of acid,
the embrace that hugs to cindered bits
your little metal envoys
and their clichés of hell,

your heaven to my hell.

Sweet sister blue, I'm a lot like you.
I too the continents, the plains,
the hills, the valleys, the yearning peaks.
Once I had seas, once maybe
I was all of ocean and life's itch.

But I too, sailing close to the Sun,
the heat-riotous carbon dioxide:
my boiling seas to dust, the dream seared . . .

Though I squint not a star now
of our mutual night, I outshine
them all, I can even cast shadows,

cast, careless Earth, a shadow on you.

LAST WORD

She, like the planet, lovely and hurt
by squalorous man, shocked the fiesta.
'Why not?' she smiled, congested with grief,
'why not just nuke the whole disaster,
let nature start again . . .?
It would be like having a good shit.'

But, they reasoned, there might not be time
for a wiser model to fumble from the wreck
before the Sun, swollen
to a red giant, and devouring its children,
gobbled up the Earth.

'Well,' she said, 'perhaps we should all
self-obliterate, leave the planet in peace
to the birds, the gorillas, the wiser whale.'

A noble abdication, but no, they said, it is
now too late: our machines, our systems—
we cannot simply walk away from them,
there'd be anarchy, melt-down, a thousand
Chernobyls, death world-wide to bird and beast:

we have made ourselves indispensable.

HELLO?

This is Neighbour One to Planet Earth—
are you receiving? We are indeed moved
by the lonely hope of your Voyager bid
insisting outward the loving simplicities
of your far from unsophisticated minds.
And to be sure—Bach, Leonardo,
Chekhov, Miles Davies, Dafydd ap Gwilym—
we are not unimpressed. We sense, however,
a reserve, a hesitation—do you receive us?—
about what you might call the crocodile within . . .

No, the craft itself has not yet arrived—
the fastest thing you have ever launched
won't snail our way for millenia yet, no—
we read your schemes on the radio waves:
in five or six hours, at the speed of light,
tonight's t.v. will zoom past your envoy and its
lumbering p.r. to deliver in bits and babel pieces
an other tale: how some Daz and Dallas,
how some crawl in the desert covered in flies,
how the happy families scream and smoulder,
snap and crackle, while ceaseless the heat
for the whitest shirt, the sexiest drink—
unanimity only when all transmitters
cut the coffee and chocs to warn of war . . .

The show so far? Chaotic yes, but vital too,
with a certain primitive originality—Mozart, Picasso—
that is not entirely devoid of interest.
Your knowledge, though, gallops beyond
your wisdom—we speak from ancient experience,
survivors ourselves of the techno-moment.
You are at a familiar turning point,
but don't expect us, who learned at last
to live with ourselves, to drop in and sort you out.

We adhere strictly to non-interference
in all internal planetary affairs,
and we fear that even a courtesy call
could tilt you into panics of self-destruction.

Do you, Earth, do you receive us?
No? Stay tuned, and endeavour to practise your own p.r.
We'll try again in an aeon or two.

MORNING STAR

On the watch, these waning days,
for moments, a sign, the
pulse of continuity . . .

such as, it seems,
these two out striding
the sea's first light,
at ancient one with,
from hairstream to heel,
all the hurt and ocean's song . . .

such as, it seems . . .

til closing they pass,
their eyes whited,
their ears locked in
tinselating headsets,
from each mouth the mime

> *we are not listening*
> *we do not hear*
> *we are not listening*
> *we do not hear*

299,792.5 KILOMETRES A SECOND

Light leaves us as it leaves the stars:
I see you as you were
a fraction of a fraction of a second ago,
sunned at the window, this bitter day,
by a light that's eight minutes out from home.
We kick heels waiting

for a sudden upturn, the happy accident
while gazing perpetually out on the past:
a quasar as it was twelve billion years back;
a face across the room
whose light hit the road
a hundred millionth of a second ago.

I think us back some years, you and I . . .
Where now, I wonder, is the light of that time?

ORBIT AND FALL

The apple grows,
learning as she larges
the moon's lesson,
counting one by one
every last terrestrial atom

til the sum totalled
breaks the charge that binds
the atoms of her stem

and she is plucked from the branch
by no more and no less
than the weight entire of planet Earth.

THE D.I.Y. UNIVERSE

You don't have to be an egghead. Simply follow
these basic instructions, and a new universe,
in less than a fraction of a second, is yours.
All you need are some everyday domestic tools,
one atom and a run-of-the-mill hydrogen bomb
(store well away from sources of ignition).
Elementary cooking or cycle repair skills,
while not essential, could prove advantageous.
Your work surface should be sound, dry and free from dust;
cover valuables, remove goldfish etc.
First isolate your atom (they are plentiful
but small: use a kitchen sieve with extra fine mesh).
Next pack your atom with four hundred million
kelvins of heat (oven gloves are recommended).
This, rather hotter than the centre of the Sun,
is beyond the range of most domestic cookers,
but your standard H-bomb should more than suffice
(in the event of malfunction seek a replacement:
DO NOT attempt to ignite with matches).
Trigger the device, stand well clear, and be prepared
for a Big Bang (ear muffs and goggles are a wise
precaution). In no time at all, if all is well,
there will burst into being, large as a pumpkin,
a full-size expanding universe, pinching off
like a bubble from the spacetime of ours.
In their own time and untouchable space there'll be
stars, maybe, and galaxies, and creatures, no doubt,
who'll grow to gaze and, wondering, come to call you
God, before trying their own atom-and-bomb trick.
Hours of fun are guaranteed, but please beware:
while no pains are spared to contrive satisfaction,
it may be your misfortune, if things go awry,
to create not a universe but a black hole.
Keep out of children's reach, and consult your dealer
at the earliest possible opportunity.

WORDS FOR INSCRIPTION ON A BENCH

Who wandered here in bits from interstellar space . . .

rest your atoms awhile on these atoms of oak,
this pennant rock, and listen in your blood
to the song of our sphere, as Wales rolls you nightward,
and the Earth roams the Way and the Way roams space
at hundreds upon thousands of miles an hour

. . . and in stillness, astronaut, walk away . . .

From **AT HOME** (in BBC Wales' *T.V. Ballads* series, 1995)

1. ROOTS

The Home Counties of England are anything but,
Said Katy who longed
For a house in a village in her grandma's Wales.
She was Berkshire born but not Berkshire bred—
The local churchyard held none of her dead.
None of her schoolpals felt they belonged
To this no-man's land bereft of tales
And cleansed, to make room for armies of yuppies,
Of all the folksy old Berkshire hard-uppies.

A home, said Katy, is more than just a house—
it's language, held ground, a sense of nation,
it's fields with names, it's shared associations,
it's cousins, aunts and chatterbox neighbours,
it's clean air, starlit nights, and worthwhile labour:
I'm tired of being rootless and unfree,
Llanrhyddid in Wales is the place for me.

So down the M4 sailed Katy to Wales.
But what should greet the bright-eyed homecomer?
Streets of second homes boarded up till next summer.

2. KITCHEN

The postmodern kitchen does not recall
The patience of milk on the blue slab,
Or the slumber of apples, or mangles and pails
And the sudsy red hand on the grimy flag.

There are clicks and whirrs, electrical purrs,
Gadgets a-gogo, thermostat routines:
Today's kitchen is a factory packed
With easy, speedy, super-wheezy machines.

29

First came the fridge that gave the pantry the chop,
Then the washer and drier, the blender, the mixer,
And the freezer that did for the corner shop,
The wall-phone, the microwave, the soda-pop fixer.

The postmodern kitchen is eco-clean—
The labels on the liquids (and even aerosols) swear it;
And underneath the stairs, stacked for recycling,
The used bottles and cans proudly declare it.

But the kitchen at night is recklessly bright:
The little red 'on' lights whose offing we forget
Keep, single-handed, whole power stations belching
And the sea on target to wipe out Bangladesh.

3. THE BOX

Long-gone winter nights ago
We'd all gather round the fire
To tell each other home-made tales
Of magic, loss, desire.

We coped with life in the home-made way
That we also coped with death:
In a box in the parlour they'd lay us out
When we'd uttered our final breath.

Now the parlour corpse is a gonner as gone
As the story-twined sooty hearth.
The only box we've room for now
Is this bright storysmith-and-a-half.

But the stories aren't much of our own making,
As nation bores unto nation:
In how many homes is this high-tech box
A coffin for the imagination?

4. HOMELESS

You're homeless, sure, if your dwelling's a box,
You're homeless if your blanket's *The Sun*,
But you can also be homeless if you live in a house
That's a mouldering, verminous run.
You're homeless if you're crammed in a crowded B & B,
You're homeless if you're rotting in 'A Home',
You're homeless if you're old and trapped downstairs,
You're homeless if you can never be alone.
You're homeless if there's no escape
From a husband who thumps you each night,
You're homeless if racists shove shit through your door,
You're homeless if you can't afford heating and light.
You're homeless if you live in fear of war
With nowhere safe to give birth,
You're homeless if there's never enough food on your
table—
Yes, the homeless are many, most of the people on Earth.

THE BALLAD OF CWM TRYWERYN

Cofiwch Dryweryn, the slogans cry
   From walls all over Wales:
Remember, then, for tomorrow's sake
   This most infamous of tales.

Three days before Christmas '55
   The Scousers delivered their gift:
They wanted the Cwm for a reservoir—
   The natives would have to shift.

[Chorus:]
So dam Wales, dam Wales for England,
   The Taffs may not like it much,
But they're snug in the pocket of the British State,
   And a lucrative soft touch.

The multitudes of Liverpool,
   Her Corporation lied,
Were desperate for water—
   Their thirst could not be denied.

Some sheep-bitten acres of soggy land,
   A failing peasant or two
Could not be allowed to stand in the way
   Of progress (and revenue).

Yes, the tricksy Sais omitted to say,
   Though Wales soon caught wind of it,
That their plans had nothing to do with thirst
   And all to do with profit.

[Chorus:]
So dam Wales, dam Wales for England,
   The Taffies won't like it much,
But they're the first to fall to Bringlish rule
   And a lucrative soft touch.

At the heart of Cwm Tryweryn lay
  The village of Capel Celyn
Where Welsh was the tongue that greeted you
  In every single dwelling.

Famed were they throughout the land
  For their poetry and song.
They kept the faith and ploughed their fields,
  And helped each other along.

'Flood Tryweryn?' they gasped at the news,
  'A barbarous, nightmare scheme . . .'
But the sight of surveyors unrolling their maps
  Was no figment of a dream.

They turned for help to their local MP
  And other Labour grandees,
But with Labour the lords of Liverpool,
  Plaid Bradwyr were deaf to their pleas.

'Do not drown our homes,' they begged
  On a demo through that great city.
Howls and curses, flying gobbets of spit
  Were the measure of Liverpool's pity.

[Chorus:]
So dam Wales, dam Wales for England,
  The Taffs may not like it much,
But with boundless faith in London control,
  They're a Parliamentary soft touch.

Democracy will take its course,
  The restless Taffs were assured:
Tryweryn's fate would be ordained
  By five (unelected) lords.

They set in Wales not a lordly hoof
  In deciding for Liverpool's Bill.
The path was now clear for England's MPs
  To gather round for the kill.

At last but too late the whole of Wales
  Awoke with anger bristling
(Except for George Thomas, Eirene White
  And the usual True Brit quislings).

From Pembrokeshire to Point of Ayr
  The refusal was full-throated,
But outnumbered as ever, our futile MPs
  Were—democratically—outvoted.

As the engines of destruction loomed
  Great meetings in Cardiff were held
Of councils, churches, parties, people—
  A congress unparallelled.

In vain they called for a scaling down,
  In vain they petitioned the Queen—
For what England desires England shall have,
  Brit imperial routine.

[Chorus:]
So dam Wales, dam Wales for England,
  The Taffs may not like it much,
But they're all for Elizabeth, Charles and Di,
  And a royalist soft touch.

Five years it took to build the dam
  And destroy the farms and village.
Not even the civilized violence of MAC
  Could put a stop to the pillage.

As MAC hit Tarmac's plant with its bombs
(To Plaid Cymru's pacific groans),
Tarmac blitzed every building in sight,
And heaped the dam high with their stones.

Not a wall, not a tree did they leave in place
Lest memories should linger;
They even evicted the dead from their graves
That no bone should point a finger.

As the river rose and flooded the cwm
Despair swamped the living departed,
And many a bungalowed, jobless refugee
Died early, broken hearted.

Never again, the Cymry swore,
Never again such shame . . .
But mad roads, dead jobs, the scourge of opencast:
The rape goes on much the same.

And will go on until we find
In our long unquiet deeps
The road that will lead us out again
From the dark where our freedom sleeps.

[Chorus:]
Until then it's dam Wales for England,
The Taffs may not like it much,
But they're snug in the pocket of the British State,
And a trouble-free soft touch.

BYZANTIUM IN ARFON

This too is no country,
at least on Saturday nights,
for old men
or a 46-year-old from Swansea
with a group of (thank god not English) students.
The young in one another's mouths,
gulls machined from the ramparts by
the blitzpop blasting from disco-bars,
the vomit-falls, the can-kicked crowded streets,
fist, yell, or yowl, commend the whole night long
whatever is youthful, loud and Welsh.

'This,' says Zach, 'is madder than Manhattan!'
As well, Zach, you're not some Mercian Mike—
they'd have you bundled into faggots
and scoffed with mushy peas
quicker than you could squawk Segontium.

This conquerors' first, most counter-Welsh of towns, this
Constantinople of the western vertex
where Rome ends and the Raj begins
is by now the Welshmost town in Wales,
exulting anew in the ancient iron
and arcane discriminations.
In the Black Boy a jilted bonker
whines at his mount as she leaves with someone else.
'Look,' she shouts back, 'Rwy'n i ffycio fo heno
a chdi y-ffycyn-fory.'

Caught in that nasal music all neglect
the dazed Yank, the inadequate Hwntw . . .

If, come Sunday, I bid their walls
a glad enough farewell
it's not to say I won't need to return
to their hard fold, this necessary north
where empires come
and empires, diolch i'r Cofis, go.

ABERGWAUN '97
(for Ozi Osmond)

Had Jemima and co. been less Brit and more Cymric
  Et un petit peu plus frolicky,
We'd be living today in a red wine republic,
  Not a moribund weak beer monarchy.

BROGARWCH

Swansea man weds Swansea bride

in Swansea:

Abertawe honeymoon

A Yank from a place called Wahoo
Came to Wales for a wet week or two.
   He hasn't got yet
   To where he wanted to get—
'The town of Mack-in-ellith near to Dolygalloo . . .'

IN/DEPENDENCE

any fish can fly

in the belly of a gull

A SWANSEA TOAST

To every burgess a burgage, to every Jack a Jackette,
Jacs bach, good ground from which to soar.

To all Jacks their acres beyond the wood,
The sun's green song and a fishy rain.

To each his nine, her ten holes, a care
For the sea, and sewin muscling their moons upstream.

To all Jacks their seven hills, peace in their homes,
South westerly winds and salubrious passage.

FANFARE I

let trumpets unleash

from forgetment's cave

the practical dream

FANFARE II

that all in green song

in all courses move

CAPITAL
(after Ionesco)

the Welsh for London is

Cardiff

POSTCARD

Came for a day:

setlo am oes . . .

THE LADY OF LLYN Y FAN FACH

There lived a widow by Mynydd Du,
  Her menfolk killed in battle,
Who sent each day her last own boy
  To the lake to mind her cattle.

One noontide as he prowled that shore
  Eating his barley bread
There danced at him from off the lake
  A sight that turned his head.

On the water's calm and glassy face,
  Combing her yellow hair,
Sat one whose dazzling loveliness
  Was a thing beyond compare.

This lady met his yearning gaze,
  He offered her his bread,
But gently she declined the gift
  And this is what she said:

'Put away your hard-baked bread,
  With that you'll win me never.'
Though straight she dived into the lake
  He swore he'd love her ever.

That night his mother bade him woo
  The maid with softer bread.
But the next day too she spurned his gift
  Though smilingly she said:

'Put away your soft-baked bread
  With that you'll catch me never.'
And as again she dived from him
  He wished her his forever.

Bread not too hard and not too soft
  Did his mother next advise,
And with it, at the lake next day,
  The farm boy won his prize.

'I'll dwell with you,' the maiden said,
  'And happy let us be,
But if with iron you strike me thrice
  You'll see no more of me.'

There burst then from the water's depths
  The father of the bride
Who dowried them with all the stock
  She could summon to her side.

'Remember, lad,' the old man said
  As the livestock streamed ashore,
'Three iron blows will drive all back
  To the lake for evermore.'

Three sons had they and happy years,
  He struck her ne'er a blow
'Til the day there was a christening
  To which she seemed loth to go.

'Hurry and fetch your mare,' said he,
  Flinging her bridle and bit.
'Ah!' cried she, as it struck her hand,
  'With iron you have me hit.'

The grief this first blow brought on them
  They edged in time aside,
'Til one day at a wedding feast
  Most piteously she cried.

'Hush!' he hissed as her flicked her arm
    With an iron-studded glove,
'Why weep you so untimely, wife,
    At a festival of love?'

'I weep,' said she, 'for bride and groom,
    And the sorrows that they'll see.
And you should weep, for twice 'tis now
    That iron has stricken me.'

The years passed by, their sons grew strong,
    And the fear he nigh forgot
That one more iron blow from him
    Would rend their good life's knot.

Then one day at a funeral
    With laughter she did flute.
To silence her he brushed her shin
    With his iron fettled boot.

'Such mirth when all is woe,' said he,
    'I cannot comprehend.'
'I laugh,' said she, 'for when folk die
    Their woes are at an end.

'But your woes have just begun,
    From you I must depart:
Our marriage contract by this blow
    Is torn, o love, apart.'

Her stock she rallied to her side
    And like a harvest queen
She led them up towards the lake
    From yard and pastures green.

All followed, even a slaughtered calf
　　And an ox-plough team of four,
All vanished then beneath the waves
　　And were seen again no more.

Her searching sons no trace could find
　　Of the lady's sudden leaving
Save, like a wound from farm to lake,
　　A furrow steeply weaving.

Then one day she appeared to them
　　As they thought they sought in vain,
And told them they should healers be
　　To relieve mankind of pain.

She passed on to her family
　　All the arts at her command,
And as doctors for generations they
　　Were famed throughout the land.

THE BALLAD OF PWLLDU HEAD

One long gone winter's time ago
  The press to Swansea came
To grab for war Welsh sailing boys
  In the King of England's name.

They say that more than ninety souls
  Were snatched from home and street
And, crammed below the *Caesar's* deck,
  Were despatched to join the fleet.

'You're off,' said Lieutenant Gaborian,
  'To lawless foreign lands.
The Parly-vous wants drivin' out,
  And the King, God bless 'im, wants hands.'

The *Caesar* sailed and her restive freight,
  So loth to leave Swansea town,
Were tied hands high to the timbers,
  And all hatches were battened down.

The ship, they feared, was a poor match
  For the tricksy Severn Sea,
And they met the swell at Mumbles Head
  With a chill of anxiety.

By Oxwich Point both wind and tide
  Were standing in her way,
So the captain turned her back to seek
  The calm of Swansea Bay.

Mumbles Head he was looking for,
  But the rocks of Pwlldu he found:
As darkness fell and the breakers crashed
  The *Caesar* ran aground.

'Save yourselves!' Gaborian roared
   To the men dismayed on deck.
Those bound below they left behind
   To perish with the wreck.

The *Caesar*, holed and boulder-wedged,
   Began to take in water,
And slow, as slow the tide rose up,
   Began the captives' slaughter.

They screamed, they stamped and pleas did shout
   Their souls, sweet God, to save . . .
But all, by dawn's departed tide,
   Was silent as the grave.

And when they held a court martial
   Gaborian was acclaimed
As he whose skills had saved the crew;
   For the ship's loss fog was blamed.

Of those who died in the *Caesar*'s hold
   Not a word in court was said.
And Pwlldu too, the summers through,
   Keeps dark about its dead.

But in winter on that naked point
   You'll find a crowd of stones
Telling of wreckage beneath the turf,
   A shipful of tyrranized bones.

BY OTHER MEANS
(i.m. Epynt, Capel Celyn, Selar, etc.)

In times gone by they ripped us off
  By the might and main of war,
But nowadays they help themselves
  Through the trickery of law.

FOUR TRANSLATIONS FROM THE WELSH OF MENNA ELFYN

1. KIDS' PLAY
(to Siân ap Gwynfor and all who occupied Carmarthen District Council's nuclear bunker)

'Kids' play!'
       the jibe, a
hoarse first-strike
at the motley band come to
squat beneath the scaffolds,
late summer drizzle snaking down
the blue fertilizer bags
that shield us from the gawpers.

Doll's house play:
a stone for a table,
a rock for a bed;
a roof we can reach through
to gather wild flowers . . .

'Peace' is the die that's cast in this game.

         *   *   *

Fields, out above 'Cwrt y Cadno',
like grease-paper spread
over iced *teisen lap*;
you two ready, a tobogan apiece,
ready for the slope, to go sliding crescendo
            downalong
                down
                    on those
rails a-screech like some new breed of bird,
each sledge unrolling
              a new-knitted scarf.

'Give it a go!'
         comes the call—
me scared of a slithery bruise-up,
but the urge, of a sudden,
for knowledge's sake, to go
               go
go rolling, ground zero, in a white explosion
                        like a snowdrop,
a snow-bell,
three snow-gems in the dust.

Yes, that's how it was, our day of
snowflakes, day full-tilt of
              whooping
                  freedom.

         *   *   *

Through today's cynic brays
thoughts surface
of then and that snow: of kids' play
before they stumble on the stone of 'commonsense'—
              play safer, it would seem,
than these bitter games,
              the games of grown-ups.

2. SHOES
(in a museum of Résistance and Nazi memorabilia)

Way-worn by Oslo
one Sunday afternoon
our feet sought out
a museum's gentler pace:
a museum of shoes,
regiments and regiments
in row on neat row
of children's shoes,
removed and set down in an orderly manner
before the little ones were gassed of an afternoon.

So bereft of meaning are shoes without feet.

Stout little shoes,
shoes with laces tied and hardly worn—
unsplashed through puddles,
unscuffed against bark,
not a toecap to bewail a fall,
no leather creased into durable smiles
by the deft percussion of tiny soles;
shoes hinting of
just-beginning-to-walk.

And that's how
there erupted this blister—
through bearing witness
one Sunday afternoon
to a people and the manner
they met their end
so noiselessly
in their stockinged feet.

3. LOVE'S SCALES

The night's pursuit of her
was nothing to the moon,
then his dark highness
flung down all his weight in a heap,
human granules,
and, lifting up a fistful of dust,
dunked a finger in to taste their blackness,
sucked of them along the dark's scales,
pressed them fearfully together, a dowry
craving warmth—and there was
no resisting night's impulsion,

the weighing and the measuring,
the releasing, decreasing, lowering, considering—
the steel scale's ancient way
of diversifying mortals, as it hurls them together
in love or in pain, gram upon gram, their flesh dissolving
on a dish above the stars' too tender chains.

The weighing, the measuring, there's no holding back the night,
our instincts too frail to deny its sortings;
the dark enfolds us, limbs quake,
the kilos huddle tight until dawn divides.

4. RAINCOAT IN ASHEVILLE

Leave home without a coat?
Not on your life—
even jaunting through a land
where a cloak would seem uncalled for
the damps of my nation
will find and drench me.

No one else was flashing a mac
or brandishing brollies,
yet the gentler the weather
the more we've reason, in our thin weeds,
to fear its sting.

How timid, I declared at the bar,
how unventuresome the Welsh.
'No one would dare leave a raincoat behind
for fear of a deluge—
still less neglect a negligée.
We like to keep dry, swaddled against
all outbreaks of flesh.'

I would if I could
undress my tribe,
flay them naked of every last stitch
and leave them dancing in the rain,
puddle-struck adventurers
levitating through a champagne monsoon.

But as a matter of dampish fact
I was caught myself
holding in Asheville's neighbourly summer
both court and coat,
black coat that in the heat
of a bluegrass moment

got left, a nylon heap, on the back of a seat.
Yes, I of the tribe of Don't-Get-Caught
was caught out with a vengeance
—'A fair rain behind her'—
as I landed back in Wales,
a girl empty-handed
praying for a storm.

HAIKU AND SENRYU

she introduces
her baby to his shadow:
he waves, it waves back

smacking lushly ashore
from the bay long becalmed
: the vanished ferry's wake

caught
on the anti-theft t.v.—
can that balding scruffy pate
be mine?

sun glares off wet slate;
fishes of wind play
the pavement pools

above the pines
Bonny Tyler's palace
outshines the moon

all paths bombed
by purple bird-splat—
time we picked the blackcurrants

tide in, skiers out
—dollar signs carved
from shore to shore

and after the rain, more drizzle:
this weather melts no jellyfish

four feet whiten
the miles of shore;
two shadows join hands

on the porch
        her empty rocker
   rocked now by the breeze

     the wind an ocean
through the high leaves   a dry one
    cackles across the yard

long love
in the white high room;
gulls out sailing
the slow blizzard

shirt thrown to compost
to be eaten as earlies
in a year or two

hands rough from work . . .
all but untouchable
the hair I finger, your skin

sweeping the cliffside's
exuberant gorse,
a kestrel's shade

'... and your address?' he asks,
phone in hand, not bothering
to write it down

in from cool dusk to
a house still warm with day's heat,
the bloom of ramsons

two men on the bus—
their noses declare them
father and son

in the long-shadowed
limestone yard: an apple, stripped
to its last red fruit

after the blizzard
way across the snow
the laughter of dogs

in the dead hallway
a whiff of scent: beauty has passed
either in or out

MISS THIRD WORLD
(from the Welsh of Hywel Gwynfryn)

The girls are all assembled—
Go to it, darlings, go!
Are the judges at their tables?
Then on, boys, with the show.
　　It's just too bad—let trumpets play!—
　　Miss Ethiopia's kept away.

They've got the lot, these lovelies,
Their glitter cuts a dash—
They bought it all in Oxford Street
For who-cares-how-much cash . . .
　　But have they, in their boudoirs curled,
　　An ear for the groans of Miss Third World?

There's white wine, red wine, salmon—
Tonight we're in Cockaigne
With trough on trough of caviar
Swilled down with pink champagne . . .
　　And Miss Third World, hey what's your lot?
　　'Two children, dead—that's what I've got.'

'I'd like to visit Hollywood
And hobnob with the stars . . .'
'I'd like to ride in Voyager
And take a look at Mars . . .'
　　What, Miss Third World, is your delight?
　　'To make it through another night.'

Miss U.S.A.'s a stunner,
Miss Spain's a lithe gazelle,
Miss Germany's voluptuous,
Miss France is *très, très belle*.
　　But one, alas, is less endowed—
　　Miss Ethiopia in her shroud.

The queen of queens is chosen!
How winsome she appears,
Outpouring as per usual
Brief crocodilish tears.
    But when, Miss Ethiopia, when
    Will your wet cheeks be dry again?

THE COLLECTOR

His friends, he called them.
Not that he'd actually talk to them, these
priceless pictures of the urban poor
—nothing, good lord, sentimental like that—
but they brought him a sense of, well,
comfort almost: the frugal meals of these people,
their pictureless walls, those hands
with scarce the strength to wield a spoon:
he wasn't, they implied, the only one
to be lonely in the world
—which he felt, oh yes, just once in a while.

And those empty gazes,
the way that their eyes seemed never to meet
the eyes of another; the way they appeared
unspoken to, unspeaking, even
among themselves, unable, it seemed,
to do a single simple thing together.
Rootless and yet . . . immobilised.
On these walls, in this house.
That was also, perhaps, in a curious and
indefinable way, not without its
consolations.

AN ASIDE FROM THE DUNGHILL
'The Prince of Darkness is a gentleman . . .'
(*King Lear* III.iv.147)

Walk on: obey: walk off:
why trouble the great tragedy
with a death like mine—
shrugged out on the dunghill,
run through from behind when I
upped and said no
to the murdering of his eyes?
The old man himself,
weeping blood at both sockets,
they flung from his hearth
to smell and fumble
his way to the coast.

Servant 1, Servant 2 . . .
Nameless men like me
are not men but shadows
and the bearers of shadow,
casting lengths of a lord
wherever he commands,
fed or beaten as our lord is liked,
the shadows of machine.
How could I have stopped them?
Better to have kept my nerve
for the job
than to end like this, my own eyeballs
pressed wide with dead pain
in the castle's shit.

But how it rattled their cosmos
when the silence I was bred for,
the yes-my-lord-no
cracked under weight
of that old man's scream.

From the womb I'd said nothing,
less the pattern of patience
than scared as beaten dogflesh
of hunger's maddening road.
They bred me to serve, to carry the cup
for their ceremony of words
and to wait, without ears,
as their large speeches
wriggled land through the banks
and eased to an early grave
lives no longer of use to the plan.
And I
did my job. I watched from the wall
as unkindness fattened
and banished plain love,
as daughterly words
grabbed a father's kingdom
and stripped from his head
the last leaf of patience.
I have seen feelingly
age punished, pity robbed,
justice to its popping eyeballs
in gold.

And I was one
of the gang sent to fetch him.
We shoved him to the room
where his guests were waiting,
and there we bound up
his corky old arms, there we
lashed him
for their hail of questions,
for my lady to tweak out
a hair from his beard.
And there it was,
against all the conventions,
that my lord himself

skewered from its socket
the scream that stripped me, that
drove me between them, thrill'd with remorse,
to prohibit their game.

It was she that stopped me,
she that stuck me from spine to belly,
shutting my upstart noise
from the scene—for her lord,
though mortally knived by me,
to jerk away
the old man's last eye.

I begin now to rot
in the strata of dung,
forgotten by the great and
bourgeois critics,
the gleeful despairers.
The curtain's down,
down and yet
I trouble the play,
voice whispers from here
that if mine were the hands,
hands under fear that
bound the old father
and viced him into pain,
mine are also the hands
that with flax and with eggwhite
laid salves on the outcast's
bleeding face;
that if ours have been the hands
obedient for lifesblood
to a dog in office
ours too are the hands
that obey nothing,
when the jackboot strides,
but the voice it crushes.

I rot into dung,
and there is good,
if you can use it,
spread upon the land.

A MOOD OF THE SUN

Thursday, they warned, Thursday's the day . . .

And Thursday is: a force twelve and rising
by dawn's upon us: those with hatches
batten, as hoardings explode
and boughs like battle-dead strew the parks.
We are unaccustomed in the cool, fed north
to such rages of wind;
even industry hesitates.

But a kid loves it, scudded down the quayside
—squat-n-leap—like a flap-wing crow,
his yelps for joy
gobbled by the banshees blown in from Eire
and raving woe through the yuppies' halyards.
I can remember
the shiver of strength down that boy's spine
as slates from a warehouse splash across his path
and unsinkables drown in the teacup marina—
the hug of tragedies not your own.

We are closer to the news than some of us know.
Thursday's advice is to stay indoors.
Indoors I stay, typing on a sheet
that even here, in this prestressed concrete
weathertight room, quivers in the wind.

ON THE BORDER, LLANYMYNECH
(for John Osmond)

Cwms ice-gouged, crags churned smooth,
ramparted, castellated, spilled and busted:
this ripped old seam of hard highland/fruity plain
is contention's cradle, from the grind pre-human
of glacial strife to a squall between neighbours
    —Taffy was a Welshman—
over something somehow seriously more
than a dodged round, the match or a girl.

    Voices at the Lion,
where I can drink in Wales and piss in England,
are a brandied agricultural gruel, wayward their slither
with Cymru's names; yet antennae long picksome
nail this transient straight as Deheubarth born
    —Taffy was a thief—
(and a *hwntw*, he must own, too dumb in *Cymraeg*
to treat even, in depth, of the weather).

Ac Offa geslog . . . swa hit Offa geslog . . .
They came yes they carved up Ynys Prydain,
they sliced us top and toe from cymric kin:
    strangers, welisc:
Offa struck with his sword the boundary out.
  And the elegies, aren't they
doing us to death? Say instead that Offa's line
marks Offa's retreat, that here at least
is where the rot stops . . . Say it, and hear it
    rattled back at you
    in the tongue of guess who
from out of our country's hollowed heart . . .

    A cheery Sais, for the camera,
straddles the line: a foot, for once, in both camps
and his balls, he laughs, in no-man's land . . .

I, called to pose, sit where I sit: for the march and its
crazings—a metre, a mile, a continent away—
    I carry within.
'Too long,' he says, 'your border so-called . . .
Not a bad try, though, fair play. But Berlin, Maastricht,
the fences are falling. It's quitsville, eh? Cornwall time,
    shopping and golf . . .
    A pint of Draig Wen?'

    Mine's a Guinness, the tart savour
of a people who dared, and a whisky to chase it
for the thistle winding free.
To memory I drink, and the burn of desire,
to bounds re-found and an end to the centuries'
    spill and blur:
that we may rise, as of old, re-made re-making,
and visioned anew for use in the world.
'You're talking,' he says, 'like some Chechen . . .'
    And so, *nos da*, perhaps I am.
I drain my glass, take a last piss in England,
    and upward gyre
to sleep among the rafters I know not where.

WIFE

She was the third to go,
the third to take with her
his latest child.

Drunk for a month, he
says he'll get a bird
—a jay or a magpie—
and he will not keep her
by caging her up,
he will not keep her
by breaking her wings.

He will keep her because
he'll take her from the nest
untravelled in the world,
and raise her, a fledgling,
to the sky of his love:
every freeing then
would return her to him.

He will keep her because
she will want to be kept.
There'll be
no caging, no ham-fisted
breaking of wings.

AMBUSH

There's certain music,
there are certain songs . . .

Winter sun,
            milklight glass,
just me sipping fruitjuice,
and a weary barmaid
waiting for time—

when *busted flat in Baton Rouge*
: a certain combination
of crotchets, minims, quavers
has me by the heart's balls,
even this cleaned-up
slush merchant job . . .

'Barperson, barperson,
whose version
is this?'

'Charley Pride,' she says, chuffed,
'My favourite tape.'

Clipped, clean, railroad rhythmics, it
certainly is
not quite Janice
but oo it's enough
to bring on you and all that sweet trouble . . .

Landlord counting money,
barmaid counting time . . .
Her tape, she says,
nearly worn out . . .

MEET ME YESTERDAY

O the lives we live without hardly our knowing . . .
I had called to you, smothered in quicksand,
and you were too busy with flying
to come, I had thought myself obliterated
by the fabulous flapping of new-found wings.

Then into this morning of accountancy and rain
there came your letter and its invitation
to a life in your life
I'd not known I'd been living:
meet me yesterday, you said:
time, you'll know it; place, a little bistro
not far from the Thames. And you welcomed me in
to your yesterday
with coffee and *very groovy* jazz,
and there I lingered, my breath you said was in you,
my eyes you could feel ensorcelling you.

And look, you said, inviting the alleged
love of your life to clamber (it was getting intimate)
right inside your brain
and compose there with you a seasonal haiku:
'As I drew on my roll-up, the wind breathed a sigh
through the last of the—'
when who should drop by,
for decorum's and orchestration's sake,
but Pablo and Raymond and the sisters Roche . . .

It was some party, yet not so sweetly loud
that I couldn't decipher
your heart's acrobatic, contradictory news.

But if, now and then, you can find me yesterday
where I thought I had no business to be,
what, I wonder, are we up to today,
and where, o wayward, might you take me tomorrow?

RENDEZVOUS

And we are not the same:

our bodies since then have
one and a half times
changed their cells:

this version of mine
has never known
that version of yours.

FOOLISH THINGS

A dozy, fog-bound
summer Sunday night,

klaxon barps blaring
down on the sea road,
a Euro-truck lost . . .

I walked behind a stranger
in yesterday's sun—
her glide, her shape, her
hand's way with a cigarette
rang risky old music

: your face turning
in the Piazza San Marco
to the violence of sea-light,
a smile at first sun-forced
completed by you . . .

Now, like tomorrow,
the latest of days,
klaxon bleating in mist
for the roads of Europe,

the good women,
the lost men.

AH, YES . . .

She'd forgotten, she said,
the sound of his voice . . .

Thinner, he found her,
slightly hungry, even—
but beautiful still, he'd
forgotten nothing.

The talk was of food, was
talk was talk . . .

Of the mould she noticed
on the inside of his boot-heel
she made no mention.

TEETOTALITARIAN LAMENT

'Pour, oh pour that booze away,'
  Said my conscience when it came to call
And spotted the dozen bottles of hooch
  I had laid up in the hall.

So I pulled the cork from bottle one
  And poured it down the sink—
Apart from just one glass of the stuff,
  A little farewell drink.

Then I pulled the cork from bottle two
  And did more or less the same,
Except this time I drank two small glasses,
  For which thirst must take the blame.

From bottle three, three glasses I took,
  From four, yes, four I drank.
Then I grabbed hold of both the bottles
  And poured 'em down the sank.

I pulled out the cork from sink number five,
  Poured the bottle down the glass and drank it,
I then pulled the sink from the cork of the next,
  Bottled seven whole pours and sank it.

From the next full sink I pulled the glass
  And bottled the cork down the pour,
I pulled the cork from my throat, the glass from the pull,
  And drank a few sinks more.

When I had emptied everything
  I steadied the house with one hand.
And counted with the other the bottles and corks—
  Some fifty at first I scanned.

I counted again when the houses came by,
  And got 'em all, about a hundred, I think—
All except for one house and a bottle
  Which I promptly proceeded to drink.

DAFYDD AP GWILYM GOES TO TOWN

Same Saturday night low expectations.
Why bother indeed
to powder the cock and pocket the lens case?
I don't even figure with the bus conductor
who stares right through me with his one good eye
and misses my fare.
Ah well, another quid
for the Double Dragon . . .

Too much boozing brings on dandruff.
Rosemary shampoo, they say, is a cure.
But I can think of a better one, cariad,
I can think of a better one.

BLUE MOON

It was blue moon time, two blue smilers in a single month,
and a go-between moth, its blue proposal
a breath between us;
in Algeria the righteous were out cutting throats,
but in July's room the windows were wide,
and while pain eyed up prospective dominions
a certain decision (what, no irony?) was asking to be made.

Yes, a breath, no (some irony, please) . . . It was you then
that made the running, you wanted a storm, a sky
of shooting stars and darts of lightning,
and of the yes of two breaths you constructed
a kiss, the kiss that has me prey, months and miles gone, to a
woman on a hill in Sir Trefaldwyn.

You made me want to sing a young man's song,
(the editor would like some irony)
and by river, in garden, in Severn Sea and on
that star-blessed hill
you sang me to a place I'd not been before
nor had had in youth the years to imagine.

The sea and a cello bloomed from within you
and I swam in the very eye of your smile;
the hurt years were a radiance, a sketch of wren's feet
dancing east and west of your lit brown gaze.
And if I loved a woman with painted toes
I also loved a girl
with knobbly knees and a basket of secrets.

Love was, yes, a red dress
(some irony, please, the editor insists)
and sometimes a denim jacket,
your sassy stride kicking out the silks.

In letters also you dressed for me
—those historic trousers—
and undressed too, naked in sunlight on your big bed,
your healing self surrounded
by sweet peas, rocket, fairies in the head,
a man somewhere and a table waiting.

And now this present of the past tense
(this poem is doomed without irony) . . .
You seemed to me awake, and I to you,
but one was asleep, one dreaming,
and look who now makes a loser's running.
Where gentle guile salts kindness
I don't know that I know what the speeches mean.
You, who have dressed in black for winter,
you are everywhere, and nowhere,
though on trains I search, in pubs and on
impossible streets, detecting, perhaps,
the ghost of your stride in a stranger's dance,
your dementing Diorella in a queue for chips,
(some irony at last, and not before time)
cod, chips and mushy peas.

THE LONG HISTORY OF A
BRIEF GLANCE

And what did we do? but walk on by,
huddle back like mutes
among the blind faces, the flags of noise—
no word between us but the dark
statement of nameless eyes: *complete stranger,*
I know you well—
then nothing of you
save a flash of heel, a breath of patchouli . . .

I've met them, such eyes,
in some sometimes of the weariest cities: they'll
reach to you in mirrors and in the passing of trains;
down vacant throughways crowded with feet
they'll come, dark eyes, to meet you
with silence, with nothing less
than their love:

and as you dance in them you dare
to lose them,
to sleep the night, like any other,
in a separate town.

In nineteen hundred and seventy six
I passed her on a stairway,
she ascending, me going down:
we, you and I, made a night of our eyes,
and in that night I touched you, we
touched beyond the moment
our innermost realms—

till the light broke us back
to move forever
away through the crowds.

Twenty years later
I close my eyes to see you, to
lose you again.
And space that emptied of you
refills with failed sunlight, begrimed marble—

the smell of patchouli warm from your skin.

EARTH LIGHTS

I

Here too, that day, upwind somewhere dead
a mammal stewing—one of us? here?—
curdling the cwm's late harvest air . . .

In beneath pines
                    —sheep? cow?—
                                        beneath
beeches filtering—horse? man?—first gold
            to the stream,

all but leapt on
                    a charred stump that
                    wasn't,
champagnes of maggot
ashimmer at the eye,
                        muzzle and vulva,

her black mare's tail for days unmoved.

II

Here, now, away again
from the stench-free news-deaths

and last night's
                    no-more-now-than-dream
                    American kisses,

the counsel of moss, of air through boughs,
the mare
            a bombed-out skeleton.

Where maggots fizzed, bloating on sludge,
heads of snowdrop hang,

                          whiter than the bone,

perfecting the dance
            of a single star.

THE GALLO-SAXON MUSE

I am a Wales-based writer,
  The English call me Welsh,
So, bless him, does my publisher
  (Not, note, *Anglo*-Welsh).

I was born, it's true, in Purley
  To a taxman and his wife,
But my ex-hubby's step-great-grandma
  Lived in Chepstow all her life.

I moved from Hove to deepest Cowbridge
  About a year ago;
Now I'm as Welsh as Kingsley Amis,
  Princess Di or Geoffrey Howe.

But I am not parochial,
  From all jingo I am free:
I write about universals—
  My garden, my cats and me.

We postmodern Wales-based writers have
  Some civilising to do
In this land of bards retarded by
  Penguin's *Hanes Cymru*.

What use is all this history,
  All these fusty, bardic arts—
Save that I seem by their reflection
  Exotic in foreign parts?

'Foreign', of course, meaning England
  Where I'd never have made the grade
Unless I'd upped sticks, dug deep for some roots
  And resurfaced, hey presto, Welsh-made.

So glide aboard the Taffy-train,
Become a Wales-based writer:
Wales and Welsh writing belong to us,
The future couldn't look brighter.

NO EXPLETIVES

It's embarrassing, you say,
you as organiser don't know quite
how to put it, but when I come to your town
to read my poems, you don't want, nudge nudge,
any expletives—ladies present, if I
get your drift, a family audience.

It is indeed embarrassing,
but you could try putting it another way,
with the tender solicitude for the second sex
of a New Man I was on a train with only last night:
'Eh, boys,' he said, 'boys,
'watch your fuckin' language, boys—
can't you see there's cunt about?'

BIRTHDAY CARD JINGLE

A birthday rhyme we send you
On this happiest of days.
It might be mostly rubbish,
But this is the stuff that pays.

There once was a fellow named Lear
Who lived neither there nor quite here,
    And a staggering propensity
    For verse of nonsensity
Had fearful but cheerful old Lear.

BOOKSHOP

I'm browsing in 'Barddoniaeth'
when up stomp two unlikely lads,
Hooch-swiggin an'
eyes a-poppin at the
lovers on the cover
of my *Acts of Union* . . .

'It's never . . .?'

'It is, mun, the fuckin works.'

'On the front fuckin cover of a fuckin book! Give it 'ere . . .
fuckin poetry . . .'

'*Fuckin* poetry . . . or fuckin *poetry?*'

'Fuckin *poetry.*'

'Fuck it.'

MILKY WAY, LLANYSTUMDWY
(for Gillian Clarke)

'You think Wales is weird? Come outside n take
a look at this . . .' The city kids from England,
    wise their teen lives
to noise-lit streets, the night-free nights, grope
down towards the garden . . .'Look at what, Gordon Bennett?'
'This.' 'What?' 'This, the sky . . .'

No moon, no street glare: crystal the dark, a silence
on us
    as eyes that heard tell but never saw
      widen to the Way,
      drink deep the milk
of our galactic home, splashed rim to chalice rim through
      disposable night

. . . two hundred thousand million suns . . .
dust, gas . . . the matter factories . . .

'I had forgotten . . .'
        'I never knew . . .'

... and Andromeda, the neighbour light
fresh to the eye as
      cold to the toes
      through wet sneakers,

on track to us
from times pre-human,
    two million light years abroad . . .

Caer Gwydion, Caer Arianrhod . . .

'What is it all?
    Where are we?'

A garden,
a garden in the Square of Pegasus,
with lamps at sea
                    and cows chomping cud,
        every few minutes the splattering of shit, a

—shooting star—

Tonight, boys and girls, we could build Stonehenge.

PORTH CWYFAN
(for Roland Mathias)

Cold June for me too, snouting round Aberffraw's fields
    for the lost llys, the rubbled
    steel that only once since then
—when all of a wonder, there, long sought, this other is,
the island parish riding aground in its *comfortless bay*,
    your froth-tormented lines made flesh.

Old Marcher bard, old no-nonsense
bridger of the crazings and shoulderer wide of rust-tight doors,
    take for your own
this pre-Cambrian chunk of sea-rolled gneiss, who wound me
    by welcome, by words unblinding
    back to the lost elementals.

I found it in a pool, as green in water as an eye or hope,
    as I stumped the mashed causeway
    to that bell-bereft
        ark of stone,
no dog to yap me, but, nipping still at respite's heels,
    the British fact, Gwynedd be damned,
of those Hawks training, for sales and votes, to murder
    a far-away nation's soul.
What more than this impotence can we call our own,
our peninsula's bedrock by plague and stormwreak weathered
                down
till we are islands to each other and dead to the world?

I stumble where you strode—choosing, seeking—the lost rockway
    from isle to isle, a bee among us.
If I know Roger Parry, fogged beneath lichen by the north wall,
    it is thanks alone to your witness,

the unrhetorised song you beamed throughout the greendays'
                                                          froth
of Luxembourg, horse shows, patchouli, grass,
    the conformities of rebellion.

It has been a work, this journey, a revolt in affirmation
    of the beseiged particularities.
    Can I name what I find
on this deck of matted couch and wind, that has and has not
sails of dunlin, pibyddion y mawn, shrilling their lone
    to the far planets?
There's a cargo here of more than bones,
though the door you walked in through, and Llywelyn and
                                                    them all,
    is locked to me.

It was all to me once, as still to most, a phantasmagorical dust,
having neither language nor yet the language
    to find in glum stone
the lubricious, scintillant life it can sing.
This dried chunk I send you of ancientmost Wales,
this monolith maquette, I raise to you now
    in the imagination,
where it stands, rain or dry, an enduring, oceanic green.

A LENGTH OF RUSTED CHAIN
(for Tony Conran)

They sang in Welsh their Saxon Reservoir: Llyn Celyn would
                                                        speak
—let by-gones be gone—not a word of English,
would breathe not a gable, not a drownèd branch
to excessively stir the memory's silts . . .
                a lake,
                a lake in Wales,
                a Welsh lake . . .
the anglers their fish, the poets, the painters their English views
and generous compensatory terms, the full mod con.

I give you, Tony, breathlessly late for your festival,
this chain plucked, in the year of heat and literature,
from the sun-crazed silt of Cwm Tryweryn,
and call, south to north, *in the iron of our chains*,
on the lightning that glints when rocks bomb in the boiling Twrch
                to fire this hand,
        to boulder down all the rivers of Wales
a restorative rage, a dam-dementing intelligence.

There are chains and there are chains. Yours of gold unites,
twines back to *the warm belonging root of us*, and sings us on.
This too unites, from Venta Silurum to Holyhead,
        link by rusted, impotent link.

        Ddys cwd bî ôl ddat wî haf lefft.

Gone, for blind profit, the stealthy copse and holy quilted fields,
gone harp and hymn,
gone the sanity of walls, the ruminant boulders,
gone bridge and drunken moon,
gone cymhortha and cynghanedd,
gone bro Tryweryn, the untranslatable, non-re-locatable life,
gone even the dead, their carcases evicted
that not a bone embarrass this murderous simplicity.

We are good at water: rivers, lakes, the dripping tap of elegy.
Beauticians of defeat, failure junkies,
we cwtsh at last into 'never again',
for Plaid Bradwyr vote ever again—
          and it's
Cofiwch Dryweryn, Cofiwch Selar, Cofiwch Olew Aberdaugleddau.

One golden day that Indian summer
I stumbled down from the fast new road to walk along the old,
and my eyes were not dry, I could find in my heart
not a sliver of postmodern irony to defend me from the history
that—rubbled, dynamited, scorched to the stump—
had lain for parched months wide to the sky:
the skeletal walls bereft of pasture; the streams gouging mud
to find again the stone of their beds;
a slate, a spoon; and here, whole, Celyn's bridge
bridging again a resurgent Tryweryn . . .
And at Hafod Fadog, in a room of air, a secret room,
I found creatures ungrasslike of silt and dew, found
where harrows had sung good heart to the field
          this crippled torc.

          Rattle it, shake it, send its cracked peal
to the malls and brasserias where the liberators doze.
Come, you deconstructivist smilers, come you requirers
that Celyn like Cymru never is, was nor ever shall be.
Come and stand on the grassed and Tarmaced heap of it all,
          feel beneath your feet
the very stones of the houses, the chapel, the school
that seasoned the packed rock of Cyrmu's damnation.

About the Yangtze dams' uprooted millions
          we deserve no say
who do not hear, for the jet-skis' narcotic whine,

our own lost—of Efyrnwy, Clywedog, Cantre'r Gwaelod . . .
    Felly, Cofiwch Dryweryn!
—and cofiwch too the carcase-worrier's sweet inertia . . .

Consuriwr, mentor, poet of our country's future tense,
may this chain I send you translate in transit
    from a thing of enslavement
    to the links that learn us unity
and like you remember, sing like you, remember tomorrow.

THE RESIDUE

Carboniferous limestone, oil:
the collective memory . . .

We nibble at light,
forge from stars dead and a living star
the cells that invite us
to linger awhile
as they die, repeat, die, repeat . . .

Though we lose in a life
—buried in carpets,
  sewered to the sea—
ten more or less material selves,
the singularities persist
: rough face and name,
guiding loves, precise guilt . . .
persist and leap each body's leaving.

Unrepeated, unrepeatable
from here to before and after all . . .
then smoke, ash,
when? blue sky, blue sky, who?

Vanished tricks of dust and light

tapping like snowflakes
at the 'lids of the living.

An Execrably Tasteless Farewell to Viscount No

The Viscount of No, Wales rejoice, is dead.
White man's Taff
And blathersome stooge of the first 'Order!'
Orgasmic in ermine,
May his garters garrotte him.

O Death! For past misdeeds I almost forgive you
Now that you've lightened our land of this load,
The Lord of Lickspit,
The grovelsome brown-snout and smiley shyster
Whose quisling wiles were the shame of Wales.

Queen-cwtshing, BritNat, Cymro Da,
The higher he climbed the acider the rain
He pissed on his people
As he stuffed them with Prince shit
And cheered as the voice of Tryweryn was drowned.

Now he's a No-vote,
His goody-buckled-two-shoes dancing aflame
In his Hell of our Yes.
The hand that crossed that paper—
All power to its arm.

Fuck me to heaven in a bath of champagne,
The rending and gnashing of the Viscount's No,
His old 'Order! Order!' 's sweet disorder
Is youth to my ears,
It's a cowin' glee-bomb.

SOME WORDS FOR ENGLISH VICEROYS, RUGBY PLAYERS AND OTHERS, IN ABUSER-FRIENDLY ENGLISH, TO HELP THEM CON TELEVIEWERS THAT THEY CAN SING THE WELSH NATIONAL ANTHEM.

My hen laid a haddock, one hand oiled a flea,
Glad farts and centurions threw dogs in the sea.
I could stew a hare here and brandish Dan's flan,
Don's ruddy bog's blocked up with sand.
Dad! Dad! Why don't you oil Auntie Glad?
Can't whores appear in beer bottle pies?
O butter the hens as they fly!

Llew Thomas

NOTES ON THE POEMS

The Cosmic Gnomes

These 'gnomic verses', or 'gnomes', in an adapted form of the *englyn penfyr*, were commissioned by Swansea City Council for incision in slate on the walls of the Tower of the Ecliptic astronomical observatory on the seafront. Ultimately, six of the eight (nos. 1, 2, 3, 5, 6 and 8) were selected to appear on slate plaques carved by the Rhydaman calligraphic artist Ieuan Rees.

Although one of the oldest of the Welsh bardic forms, a famous example being the ninth century lament 'Stafell Cynddylan' (Cynddylan's Hall), it seemed an appropriate model for a commission touching on both cosmological and human affairs. For the early Welsh nature gnomes, which combine the classification of natural phenomena with aphoristic wisdoms, represent perhaps the beginnings of science.

The Welsh gnomic stanza is sometimes compared with a somewhat better known three-liner, the Japanese *haiku*. Concision, observational accuracy and a strict syllable count are features common to both forms, but they differ in important respects. The more youthful *haiku* is concerned with particular times and places, and will have nothing to do with proverbial utterances, whereas the gnome is a sententious statement about universals.

Characteristics of the *englyn penfyr* include a syllable count of 10, 6, 7 (sometimes 8) per line, a rhyme between the second and third lines, and, when the *englynion* appear as a chain of stanzas, a continual light touching on a single idea at the beginning of each verse. The first part of a traditional gnome, often the first two lines, is descriptive—usually of nature; it concludes with a line of folk philosophy.

The poet Menna Elfyn who translated my English originals into Welsh has imbued her *gwirebau* with strong and mellifluous elements of *cynghanedd*, the ancient system of sound-chiming within a line of verse.

The figures separating each pair of gnomes are hieroglyphic representations of a planet, the human hand and a star. In Ionia in the Aegean Sea, the birthplace of science 2,500 years ago, the hand was revered as the agent of intellect and the means whereby the Ionians, who were the world's first atomists, could reveal the order ('cosmos') behind the supposed chaos of their universe.

299,792.5 Kilometres a Second
is the speed of light.

The Ballad of Cwm Tryweryn
'Cofiwch Dryweryn' means 'Remember Tryweryn'. 'Sais' means 'Englishman'. 'Plaid Bradwyr' means 'the party of traitors'; 'Bradwyr', of course, chimes with 'Llafur', meaning 'Labour'. 'Cymry' means 'the Welsh'.

Byzantium in Arfon
—with apologies to W.B. Yeats, author of 'Sailing to Byzantium'. Ancient tradition associates Caernarfon, or Segontium, the Romans' most westerly legion post, with the eastern capital of the Roman Empire. Caernarfon's old name, Caer Cystennin (Constantine's Fortress), was also the name used for Constantinople, and Constantine himself was believed to have been born at Segontium. '*Rwy'n i ffycio fo heno/a chdi y-ffycyn-fory*' means 'I'm fuckin' 'im tonight/and you to-fuckin'-morrow!' '*Diolch i'r Cofis*' means 'Thanks to the people of Caernarfon'.

Abergwaun '97
Jemima Nicholas (d. 1832), according to the legendary interpretation of 'the Last Invasion of Britain' at Strumble Head near Fishguard, or Abergwaun, in 1797, is supposed to have frightened the republican French into submission with the aid of a crowd of local women.

Brogarwch
means 'love of the home patch'.

A Swansea Toast
was commissioned by Swansea City Council as part of a (controversial and uncompleted) city centre poetry project on the theme of 'The Magic of Place'. It was inscribed in metal and stone in Oxford Street, Swansea in December 1992.

Fanfare I, Fanfare II
Both fanfares were commissioned by Swansea City Council for incision in a wall in Singleton Street, Swansea, 1989-90.

Postcard
was commissioned in 1996 by the City and County of Swansea Council and the Family Housing Association (Wales) Ltd. for the walls of a new building in Christina Street, Swansea where the second phrase ('setlo ar fyw'n fodlon') differs slightly from the version here, 'setlo am oes', which means 'stayed a lifetime'.

The Lady of Llyn y Fan Fach
One of the most famous of all Welsh legends, first told to me by my paternal grandmother whose family came from nearby Llangadog.

The Ballad of Pwlldu Head
In November 1760 a pressgang came to Swansea looking for Welshmen to fight in England's 'Seven Years War' against the French. This is the true story of what happened on that occasion. I am indebted to Wally Jenkins for most of the details.

On the Border, Llanymynech
This poem was commissioned for the 1990 *Sunday Times* Hay on Wye Festival of Literature, and begun in the Red Lion at Llanymynech, half of which lies in England and half in Wales. A '*hwntw*' is what people in north Wales call those in the south, 'them down by there'. The quotes in Old English, '*Ac Offa geslog*' and '*swa hit Offa geslog*', are from the seventh century poem *Widsith*, which tells the story of an Offa who was a king in Sleswig and an ancestor of the Mercian Offa, who moulded his life on the saga hero of Sleswig; the phrases mean, respectively, 'But Offa got by slaying' and 'as Offa struck it out'. 'Welisc', meaning 'strangers', is what the invaders called the *Cymry* when they boxed them away behind Offa's Dyke and declared them foreigners in their own land. '*Draig Wen*' refers to the white dragon of the Saxons.

The Gallo-Saxon Muse
Penguin's *Hanes Cymru* is John Davies's masterful *A History of Wales*, available in Welsh and English.

Bookshop
'*Barddoniaeth*' refers to the bookshop's Poetry section.

Milky Way

'Caer Gwydion' and 'Caer Arianrhod' are Welsh expressions for the Milky Way.

Porth Cwyfan

This poem, about the bay in Ynys Môn of Porth Cwyfan and its islanded church of Llangwyfan, refers to a poem of the same title by Roland Mathias. There is a reference in the third verse to the role of RAF Valley in training pilots of the Indonesian air force to fly British-made Hawk jets, which have been used genocidally against the people of occupied East Timor.

A Length of Rusted Chain

This poem refers to the destruction of Cwm Tryweryn by Liverpool Corporation in the late 1950s and early 1960s (see 'The Ballad of Cwm Tryweryn' on p. 32 for details). The two italicised quotations are from the poetry of Tony Conran.

An Execrably Tasteless Farewell to Viscount No

Somewhat after the Irish, via Patrick Galvin, of Séan Ó Murchadha na Raithíneach, 1700-62.